MANCHESTER

FROM THE ROBERT BANKS COLLECTION

MANCHESTER

FROM THE ROBERT BANKS COLLECTION

JAMES STANHOPE-BROWN

The History Press

This book is dedicated to the memory of Sylvia

First published 2011

The History Press
The Mill, Brimscombe Port
Stroud, Gloucestershire, GL5 2QG
www.thehistorypress.co.uk

© James Stanhope-Brown, 2011

The right of James Stanhope-Brown to be identified as the Author
of this work has been asserted in accordance with the
Copyrights, Designs and Patents Act 1988.

British Library Cataloguing in Publication Data.
A catalogue record for this book is available from the British Library.

ISBN 978 0 7524 6013 0

Typesetting and origination by The History Press
Printed in Great Britain

Manufacturing managed by Jellyfish Print Solutions Ltd

CONTENTS

ACKNOWLEDGEMENTS

I am indebted to the following people and organisations for their help in making this book possible: Chris Makepeace; National Maritime Museum, Greenwich; Manchester Libraries and Local Studies; Blackpool Central Library and in particular Dave Weedon; Saddleworth Museum and in particular Peter Fox; Oldham Local Studies and Archives; Victorian Image Collection: www.victorianimagecollection.co.uk; Liverpool Maritime Museum; Shirley A. Birch; Jonathan Duggan-Keen.

Thanks also to anyone else I may have inadvertently overlooked; your help was greatly appreciated.

INTRODUCTION

Robert Banks was born in 1847 at a time when photography was becoming fashionable, and, to someone like Robert, whose interest had been captivated at an early age, the timing could not have been better. Still in its infancy was the 'carte de visite', and, with the postcard era yet to materialize, what better opportunity for someone with the right determination to take advantage of this growing trend. As a result of his asscoiation with the *Oldham Chronicle* and the Oldham Photographic Society – Samuel Beverley in particular – Robert opened his first photographic studio shortly before his twentieth birthday. While being the first to establish a photography business in the woollen town of Uppermill, he soon realised that his dreams of a future empire in and around his home town had become somewhat limited so, in 1873, with expansion firmly at the forefront of his dreams, he moved his family to the 'cottonopolis' city of Manchester in order to fulfil his ambitions.

Robert was one of five children born to Richard and Hannah Banks, three of whom were brothers, Thomas, Alexander and Richard, and a sister named Mary. As a journeyman carpenter, Richard senior sought work wherever he could find it, which is why the family moved from Broughton in Salford to Bedford, a suburb of Leigh in Lancashire. It was there, on 2 January 1847, that Robert was born. From what little information is available, it would appear that when Robert was aged nine or ten, the family relocated once more, this time to the West Yorkshire town of Greenfield, where Richard senior had found work at a local woollen mill. At the age of fifteen, Robert is recorded as being employed as a 'woollen piecer' along with his younger brother and sister. Unfortunately, there is no further record of Robert until his twentieth birthday, by which time he had become an 'illustration artiste' for the *Oldham Chronicle*. Obviously talented, and influenced by friends in the Oldham Photographic Society, he decided to embark on a career in photography.

In 1867, Robert made two life-changing decisions. Firstly, he handed in his notice with the *Oldham Chronicle* in order to start trading as a photographer, and, secondly, he married his childhood sweetheart, Emma Buckley, whom he had met whilst working at the woollen mill. On Christmas Eve at Uppermill Registry Office, a week before Robert's twenty-first birthday, his eighteen-year-old bride became Mrs Robert Banks.

Having traded successfully for five years from his Uppermill (High Street) studios, Robert made the decision to move to Manchester in 1873, where, along with his family, which now included a son named Agnew and a daughter named Annie, he settled at No. 73 Alexandra Road, Moss Side. Soon after this move he began renting premises at No. 73 Market Street, Manchester; a location that not only enabled him to take full advantage of the ever increasing passing trade, but also the chance to become Manchester's leading commercial photographer.

Within three years of starting his Manchester business, Robert recieved a commission from the city council to photograph the entire structure – inside and out – of the newly-built Manchester Town Hall, an achievement that followed an earlier offer to produce a photographic record for the West Yorkshire Rifle Vounteers. Another house move to numbers 80/82 Alexandra Road was Robert's idea of incorporating his family home alongside his new headquarters, a venue which he aptly named 'Rembrandt House'.

Over a period of forty years trading in Manchester (1874-1914), the Banks family rented a total of fourteen different studio addresses around the city; from Market Street to New Cross, Fountain Street to Victoria Street, and Alexandra Road to Mytton Street, Hulme, the latter bearing the name 'Opal House'. In his quest to be at the forefront of any opportunity, Robert created an outlet at the seaside town of Blackpool, where, for three years or so, he competed with like-minded photographers for a share of the booming carte de visite trade. As well as renting a studio in Talbot Square, he also traded at Blackpool's North Shore and South Shore.

While acknowledging his entrepreneurial genius, Robert Banks can best be summed-up as someone whose motives were financial reward and fame, although sadly, today, he is still comparatively unknown. Unlike some of his associates, Robert was a 'people and events' photographer, a man-of-the-moment character who strived to be at the forefront of any worthwhile and important occasion – as revealed in the pages of this book. Not only was he a master with the camera, Robert was a man who had his fingers on the pulse of the city's heartbeat, chronicling for posterity the turning tide of change between the nineteenth and twentieth centuries. During his career in his adopted Manchester, Robert is thought to have produced hundreds of carte de visite's, which, together with his commercially produced postcards, formed the basis of his photographic empire. Never one for marking time, Robert also produced several photographic albums, some of which include the opening of the Manchester Ship Canal, the London Lord Mayor's official visit to the city, the unveiling of Queen Victoria's statue, and King Edward's visit of 1909, when he opened the Mancheter Royal Infirmary, an occassion that earned Robert an official 'By Royal Command' title.

Over many years I have tried to trace Robert's final resting place, a search which took my enquiries to Australia, Canada and the United States. However, after following up a final lead, I recently discovered his burial plot in the North Wales town of Colwyn Bay, and, unbelievably, his precious name sign, 'Rembrandt House'.

It is hoped that Manchester will one day recognise the part Robert Banks played in the city's history and include him alongside Manchester's illustrious greats.

James Stanhope-Brown, 2011

1

WHITSUNTIDE WALKS

When it came to photographing Manchester's Whitsuntide Walks, it would appear that Robert Banks held the monopoly, especially during the early years of the twentieth century. His postcards of these events, another major source of income for him, became very popular not only for their quality, but because of the affordable rate of postage on postcards as opposed to letters. The photographs were also popular amongst those who kept family albums and records of their church's annual Whit Walks and, for those whose faces appeared on the finished product, the rare opportunity to become an overnight celebrity. As an example, this photograph, showing the Roman Catholic Walks along Piccadilly, depicts a contingent from the Italian population who resided in Ancoats, and there is little doubt that anyone in this photograph would have gone unrecognised.

The contrast of the white dresses of these Sunday school teachers against the city's blackened Piccadilly Infirmary could not be more stark.

Another unidentified group of church representatives marching along the Piccadilly esplanade in the direction of the Queen's Hotel. On the right of this picture is the familiar building of the Midland Railway Company.

This group of women with a large banner are walking along Princess Street near the Town Hall. The photograph must have been taken in 1906 because the writing on the banner lists the years as 1896 to 1906. The heading on the banner refers to the Mary Jones Union. One assumes that the Mary Jones Union was connected to the Bible Society because of the society's foundation links to a young Welsh girl called Mary Jones.

The dresses and outfits worn by these children are absolutely breathtaking, especially when you consider the sacrifices made by working parents to make/buy them. In some households it was normal practice to scrimp and save for a whole year, and even go without food in order to dress their offspring for the Whitsuntide Walks. This photograph was taken on Princess Street at the turn of the century.

Dean Edward McClure (marked with a cross) leads this Whitsuntide contingent of Manchester Cathedral clergy.

Apart from the known fact that this photograph was taken on Piccadilly, there is no indication as to who these well-turned-out girls represent. Are they Monday walkers, or are they Friday walkers?

Believed to have been taken in 1906, this photograph shows the Whitsuntide Walk contingents as they gather en masse in Albert Square. It is obvious that many hours of planning would have been required in order to stage such a monumental procession but, as history has proved, the successes of the 'walks' speak for themselves.

It was not unusual for the Whit Walks to be affected by the Manchester weather. However, as this photograph shows, this was one of the better years. In this postcard view, the immaculately dressed banner-carrying girls are walking along Piccadilly, having just passed the Albion Hotel.

Unfortunately there are no clues as to which denomination these Princess Street 'walkers' belong to, but this photograph does portray the kind of dedication that was generally applied to all Whitsuntide walkers.

Row after row of walkers! What a wonderful sight it must have been as a bystander, observing all the pageantry that was associated with the festival. Since Queen Victoria's statue is included with the other Piccadilly statues, it is obvious that this photograph was taken after 1902. Again, the clues as to which contingent the 'walkers' belong to are unavailable, but to compensate there is a wonderful view of the Piccadilly Infirmary.

This picture shows the 1905 Mary Jones Union 'walkers' parading along a different section of Manchester's Princess Street.

What a beautiful picture for the proud parents of these little girls who belong to the Salford church school of St Stephen's. The banner reads: 'Faith – The Fathers – The Children'.

When Robert Banks took this Whit Walk photograph in 1906 he made certain that his advertising sign was well and truly visible. His studio at that time was on the top floor of the Royal Hotel building on Market Street. The businesses below him were Broadhurst and Co. India rubber manufacturers, and Manchester Warehousemen Clerks Provident Association.

For a child to look professionally turned out was the dream of every parent, and yet it must be remembered that the majority of costumes on display were made at home, using whatever means were available.

Believed to be a part of the St Michael's of Ancoats contingent, these 'Little Italy' Italians walk proudly along Piccadilly carrying their eye-catching effigy. Clearly seen in the background is the Royal Hotel, with the Manchester Infirmary to the left and Oldham Street to the right.

This 1904 photograph is a good example of how parents and schoolteachers strived to present the best-dressed children of the Whitsuntide Walks. The St John's referred to on the banner no longer exists, but there is a garden near Granada Television studios which commemorates the former Deansgate church. Of note is the fact that by the end of the Whitsuntide celebrations, the city centre businesses – those that stayed open – would have increased their turnover by a hundredfold. However, the outright winner of the competing business outlets would have been the brewery, whose vast empire of city centre pubs provided every opportunity to relieve the working man of his week's wages.

2

THE MANCHESTER
SHIP CANAL

Seen here in 1901 is the *Flying Whirlwind* tugboat escorting a Manchester-bound cargo ship down the Manchester Ship Canal. In contrast to the name of the tugboat, there is an undeniable majestic serenity as the lumbering giant glides slowly through the calm pond-like waterway.

The Liverpool-registered cargo ship *Truthful* waits patiently at the Irlam Locks on the Manchester Ship Canal.

An aerial view of the Manchester and Salford docks, taken from the grain elevator on the Manchester side.

Very appropriately, the name of this steamship lying at the Foreign Animals Wharf on the Manchester Ship Canal is the *Manchester City*. Regrettably, only one of the accompanying tugboats can be identified. Its name is *Mercia*, Manchester.

When Queen Victoria performed the opening of the Manchester Ship Canal on 1 January 1894, her vessel was supposed to have had an escort of two Royal Navy gunboats, the *Speedy* and the *Seagull*. However, due to their size and lack of manoeuvrability, the St Anne's lifeboats took their place. Of special note is the fact that soon after the Queen's visit, the SS *Finsbury* sailed to Manchester via the Ship Canal with the first-ever cargo of cotton.

In the centre of this photograph, taken on the Manchester Ship Canal, is a schooner with the name *Christina Davis*. It was built at Whitehaven, Cumberland in 1865 and spent most of its working life tooing and froing across the Irish Sea. On 29 April 1918, she was captured by a German submarine and sunk by gunfire with no loss of life. To the left of the schooner is a two-funnel three-mast tugboat by the name of *Pathfinder*.

During the Easter celebrations of 1901, the Lord Mayor of Manchester gave a warm welcome on behalf of Manchester and Salford to the ratings and officers belonging to the flotilla of eight torpedo-boat destroyers, which were on an official visit. This photograph shows the arrival of one of the gunboats at Mode Wheel Lock.

On 29 April, the flotilla, having filled-up with Welsh coal, set sail from Trafford Wharf for their journey to Kingstown. Before departing, Commander Lloyd of the HMS *Leven* thanked the people of Manchester and Salford for their hospitality. The other gunboats in the group were: HMS *Locust*, *Wolf*, *Panther*, *Leopard*, *Gypsy* and *Fairy*.

3

THE LONDON MAYOR'S VISIT TO MANCHESTER, 1901

The Lord Mayor of London, Alderman Frank Green, visited Manchester at the invitation of Manchester's Lord Mayor, Councillor Thomas Briggs, in August 1901.

Following the death of Queen Victoria, custom demanded that every Mayor and Lord Mayor of every town, city and borough in the UK were required to present themselves to the new monarch and to swear on behalf of their respective city councils their allegiance to the new King. It was while carrying out his duty on behalf of the city of Manchester that the Lord Mayor, Councillor Thomas Briggs, persuaded his London counterpart to stay over in Manchester before attending the great Glasgow Exhibition.

As a result, the state visit of Alderman Frank Green, Lord Mayor of London, together with Alderman W. Vaughan Morgan and Alderman J. Lawrence MP, on the 2nd and 3rd of August 1901, brought to Manchester a spectacle that had seldom been witnessed. The many thousands of onlookers who lined the route were able to observe the magnificent splendour and pageantry from the moment the parade left London Road railway station. Of the three coaches bound for the Town Hall, the first contained Mr and Mrs (Sheriff) Lawrence, while the second coach accommodated Mr (Sheriff) Morgan and Mrs Hornsby-Steer. In the third gilded and glass-panelled coach, which was drawn by four horses, was the Lord Mayor of London, along with his sword bearer, his mace bearer and the Town Clerk of Manchester. On arrival at the Town Hall, the city's Lord Mayor, Thomas Briggs, welcomed the guests.

Following a civic luncheon, the party, in all its regalia, set off for the Royal Exchange in Cross Street, where, soon after, they resumed their journey to the Pomona Dock in Trafford Park, and to the waiting ship *Sapphire*. The afternoon boat trip on the Manchester Ship Canal went as far as the Barton Aqueduct, after which the guests returned to the city for a banquet at the Town Hall. On the second day of the visit, the resplendent horse-drawn coaches set off with their occupants from the Queen's Hotel in Piccadilly and, following a journey along the Chester Road, arrived at the Altrincham Works of Linotype at Broadheath. The London Lord Mayor, having laid a foundation stone for the new extensions, then continued his journey to the British Westinghouse Works at Old Trafford, where a similar ceremony took place.

In the following sequence of photographs, the London Lord Mayor's visit begins with his arrival at London Road station and continues until its conclusion at the Westinghouse Works at Old Trafford.

Opposite above: Following their arrival at Manchester's London Road station, the Lord Mayor of London, Alderman Frank Green, and his entourage receive a huge welcome from the waiting crowds prior to their tour of the city.

Opposite below: The leading coach is escorted down Piccadilly in the mid-morning sunshine. To the left-hand side of the mounted policemen is the White Bear Hotel, while next to that is the well-known Manchester firm of Seymour Mead and Co.

In this Albert Square photograph, taken in front of the Town Hall, Alderman Frank Green, Lord Mayor of London, is officially welcomed to Manchester by the city's Lord Mayor, Thomas Briggs.

Despite the distraction to the right of this picture, made obvious by the looks on the faces of the flunkies, Robert Banks manages to capture this all-important view of the two Lord Mayor's.

As the London Lord Mayor's coach rounded the corner at the junction of St Ann's Square, the waiting bystanders were alleged to have surged forward in order to view the glass coach close up.

Seen here is the magnificent 'coach and four' as it waits outside the Manchester Royal Exchange during the official visit.

Following their luncheon at the Town Hall, the VIP guests follow the route towards the Manchester Ship Canal.

In the pale afternoon sunshine, and amidst the smoke from the many ship's funnels, the guests and other invited visitors wait patiently for the start of their historic journey aboard the *Enchantress*. This scene was captured at the Mode Wheel Locks on the Manchester Ship Canal.

The foundation-stone laying ceremony taking place at the Broadheath works of Linotype at Altrincham.

This photograph was taken from Lady Kelvin Road during the stone-laying ceremony at Broadheath.

This delightful picture shows the coaches waiting outside the Linotype Works at Broadheath. To the rear of the Lord Mayor's coach is a Manchester horse-drawn bus, which had been hired to convey the many guests.

In this view, the London and Manchester Lord Mayors are engaged in the official opening ceremony at the British Westinghouse Works at Old Trafford.

4

MANCHESTER
STREET SCENES

As Manchester's leading photographer of the Victorian era, Robert Banks received many requests and commissions to photograph street scenes in and around the city, a format that proved to be of great financial benefit, especially during the early 1900s boom years of the postcard era. The following fourteen Manchester views represent just a small sample of his huge repertoire.

Believed to have been taken from the Ryland's building in 1904, this remarkable view of Piccadilly shows not only the horse-drawn and electric tramcars, but also the gloomy backdrop of Manchester's ageing Infirmary. Of note is the Queen Victoria statue, which, as yet, appears to have been unaffected by the city's grime.

Looking majestic in every way is the Manchester Town Hall, which, in the absence of any traffic, takes on an even more spectacular pose. Robert Banks and the new Manchester Town Hall both began their careers within two years of each other.

This view of Market Street, looking towards Deansgate, shows the junction at Cross Street and Corporation Street. The building in the distance on the right of the photograph is the Victoria Hotel.

Judging by this 1905 photograph of Manchester's Market Street, horse-drawn vehicles were still very much in vogue.

In this view of the Manchester Assize Courts, which lay directly in front of Strangeways Prison, a horse-drawn coach complete with footmen draws into the driveway of the main entrance. No doubt it is conveying one of the High Court judges.

Manchester's fashionable and upmarket St Ann's Square has had an association with taxi ranks going back many years. In this Edwardian view of the Square, it is possible to pick out a variety of the horse-drawn hansom cabs going about their business.

The two main features which stand out most in this turn-of-the-century photograph are the modern electric tramcars alongside the horse-drawn cab, and, the size of the newssheets being sold by the newspaper seller!

Another view of Exchange Station Approach, with the Cheetham Hill tramcars ready and waiting by the Cathedral. The statue of Oliver Cromwell became a well-known meeting place over the years.

In what appears to be a normal daytime scene on Oldham Street in 1904, a smartly dressed young girl is seen making her way towards Piccadilly. To the right of the picture is the well-known Manchester bookshop of Abel Heywood & Son, and next to that is a Marks & Spencer's Bazaar.

This photograph shows Oxford Street in the early 1900s. It would appear that Robert Banks positioned his camera at the middle of the busy junction of Whitworth Street, adjacent to the building now known as The Palace Theatre.

5

THE MANCHESTER
MARATHON WALKS

Along with the advent of the new twentieth century came great changes in the way that the working population utilized their spare time. With the countryside and seaside becoming more accessible due to the arrival of the railway, and with an increasing interest in sporting and leisure pursuits, particularly in the North West, it was hardly surprising that amongst the limited options, pedestrian walking came out on top. While cycling was still out of reach for the masses, and the motorcar almost certainly beyond the means of the working class, it was pedestrian walking that, in the absence of any financial cost, became the most supported of any pastime. For next to nothing, it became possible for an ordinary person to achieve notoriety overnight, and, in the words of the organisers, 'offered the participants the unique benefit of fresh air and healthy exercise, and above all, the opportunity to escape the suffocating smoke and grime of the city.'

By 1904 the membership of the Pedestrian Club had grown to several hundred and, included in its itinerary was an annual Whitsuntide walk from Manchester to London. However, in terms of achievement and fame, the greatest challenge lay in winning either the Manchester to Blackpool Marathon or the Manchester to Southport Marathon. The starting point for these marathons was the Albert Street Police Yard (now a multi-storey car park) which was situated at the back of Deansgate. The finishing line for both marathons was Talbot Square in Blackpool (in front of the Yates Wine Lodge) and the Lord Street Town Hall in Southport.

Following starters' orders, the marathon walkers emerge from the main gates of Albert Street Yard. Unfortunately there is no clue as to whether this was the Blackpool or Southport Marathon.

Judging by the photograph, it would appear that the starters' orders have just been announced, and that the individually numbered contestants are raring to go. Also in the running are the manufacturers of 'Oxo', who, with their advertising, have taken advantage of a great opportunity.

En route to Southport, this marathon leader receives refreshments from one of the officials. Note the sponsor's flag accompanying the race officials.

As elusive as ever, apart from the tell-tale horse-drawn carriage which carries his business sign, is the photographer Robert Banks. Captured in this photograph during the Southport Marathon is this delightful pose by the race officials.

Photographed as they approach the village of Standish are four of the Southport Marathon walkers.

These two Manchester contestants are J.E. Rankin (no. 45) and J. Brown (no. 30). By the looks of things, they are being scrutinized by the timekeepers and judges during their Manchester to Blackpool Marathon walk.

Arriving at the finishing post in Talbot Square is the proud winner of the Manchester to Blackpool pedestrian marathon. The winner, Mr Butler, is accompanied by the top-hatted medical official, Dr Howe.

The long, gruelling walk is over, and the winning contestants arrive at Southport Town Hall after completing the Manchester to Southport Marathon. Of the two Manchester men, Mr A. Ormrod was declared winner, while in second place was Mr J.E. Rankin.

6

ROYALTY

During what was to be the last year of her life and reign, Queen Victoria made a final visit to Ireland during April 1900. Seizing this opportunity, Robert Banks paid a visit to Holyhead in order to compose a photographic record of the Queen's visit. Following the successful accomplishment of the project, he produced a set of three albums, one of which he personally delivered to Windsor Castle, for it to be handed to the Queen.

In this photograph of the Royal Yacht, Robert Banks was able to capture this view of Queen Victoria prior to her disembarkation. With her Ladies-in-Waiting standing close by, Abdul Karim, her ever-faithful Indian servant pushes her along in her wheelchair.

The Rifle Volunteers of the Welsh Regiment are seen here presenting arms as Queen Victoria comes ashore at Holyhead.

On 23 January 1901, a telegram arrived in Manchester from Osborne House. The message read: 'My beloved Mother has just passed away surrounded by her children and grandchildren.' It was signed 'Albert Edward.' A quote from a Manchester newspaper that same day read: 'The longest recorded reign in British history has come to an end, and for the moment we can only feel that a great light has gone out of the world.'

Following the last strike of eleven o'clock at Manchester Town Hall on 25 January 1901, the Lord Mayor, Councillor Thomas Briggs, climbed onto a constructed platform in Albert Square in order to read out the new King's (Edward VII) proclamation.

The Town Hall ceremony, which was attended by many thousands, concluded with a resounding 'God Save The King'. Note all the hats worn by the crowd.

After concluding the Albert Square ceremony, the Lord Mayor then led his entourage to Swan Street at New Cross, where he repeated the proclamation. For the third time that day, a third performance was re-enacted on the Piccadilly Esplanade where, as seen in this photograph, many thousands gathered in front of the Queen's Hotel. A final and concluding ceremony took place later in the afternoon at All Saints' Church on Oxford Road.

A memorial service honouring the late Queen took place at the Manchester Cathedral on 2 April 1901. The procession which began at the Town Hall, included: The Mounted Police, 3rd Lincolnshire detachment, Yeomanry, Manchester Artillery, 2nd, 4th and 5th Volunteer Brigade Manchester Regiment, 3rd Volunteer Brigade Lancashire Fusiliers, City Police Band, Police, Fire Brigade and Civil Representatives and, finally, the various Consular Representatives.

This photograph shows the suitably dressed foreign consuls from the various city-centre consulates, walking along Victoria Street towards the Cathedral. Note all the spectators on the top deck of the buses.

The coronation of King Edward the seventh in August 1902 was an event that attracted visitors from all over the world, and particularly from within the British Empire. Manchester's contribution to this special occasion was much the same as every other town and city in Britain, except that is for one unusual episode which, had it not been for Robert Banks's foresight, would have ended-up as just another statistic of yesteryear.

On their journey south, in order to attend the London Coronation, a tally of 600 Indian troops, having left Liverpool, sailed down the Manchester Ship Canal for a brief stopover in Manchester. Once re-assembled, the 600 militiamen, under the command of Colonel Dawson, then proceeded to march from the Pomona Dock for an impromptu parade through the city of Manchester. The contingent was a representation of the many regiments throughout the Indian continent, which included: Sikhs, Ghurkhas, Cavalry Guides, Lancers, Viceroy Bodyguards and Bombay Grenadiers. Also included were thirteen regimental cooks and four regimental barbers.

Reportedly, the city of Manchester burst into great excitement as soon as the red uniforms had been spotted, and, from that moment on, the streets, already overflowing with homeward-bound workers, became gridlocked for well over two hours. Over the course of the following two days, individual detachments of Indian troops visited such places as: Belle View Gardens, Armstrong Whitworth & Co., Beyer Peacock's, the 'turkey-red' manufacturers of F. Steiner, the Thomas Houldsworth works at Reddish and the Manchester Technical Schools.

Opposite above: Having left the troopship *Hardinge* at Liverpool, the Indian militiamen were then directed to the two waiting Birkenhead ferryboats, *Claughton* and *Mersey* where, after being split into two separate contingents, they began their 'canal' journey to Manchester.

In the absence of any identifying features, one can only guess at which ferryboat this one is. However, there may be a clue from the advertising notice. It reads: 'Fare To and From Liverpool and Rock Ferry – one penny. New Ferry – two pence'. With regards to the Indian troops on deck, imagine what must have gone through their minds as they prepared themselves for the English climate.

Opposite below: While there are smiles for the cameraman from the troops on the upper deck of this Birkenhead ferryboat, the lower deck contingents ready themselves for their Manchester disembarkation, as yet unaware of the impact they are about to make on the city.

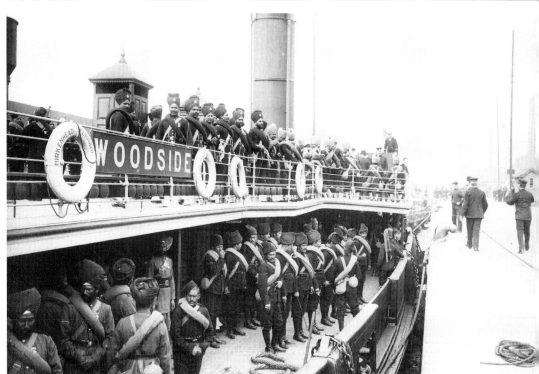

After having taken Manchester by storm, these Indian troops are seen taking a breather inside the humbling backdrop of a Deansgate police compound. Following the finale of the two-day visit, every soldier was handed a bottle of soda water, fruit, and a packet of cigarettes before leaving by train for their London destination.

M R. R. Banks has had the honour of executing work for members of the Royal Family, the Aristocracy, and many prominent personages.—Among these he may mention Her Majesty the Queen, and members of her family; many Dukes, Duchesses, Earls, Countesses, Lords, and other titled Gentry and Ladies; the Right Hon. W. E.. Gladstone, M.P.; Madame Adelina Patti, etc., etc. From many of them he has received the most flattering Testimonials as to the quality of his work.

In addition to these, almost all the Illustrated Papers in Great Britain have reproduced Mr. Banks' pictures in their columns, and have expressed very high commendation of the Artistic Excellence of all his productions.

As a mark of respect for the late Queen, and with an even greater admiration for the guest of honour, the population of Manchester turned out in their thousands to welcome the most decorated soldier ever to visit their city, Field Marshall Lord Frederick Sleigh Roberts, VC. As well as officially unveiling Onslow Ford's statue of Queen Victoria, his other engagements in the city included a tournament at the Hulme Barracks and a presentation of medals to veterans of the Crimea War.

In a series of photographs commemorating Lord Robert's visit, Robert Banks's took advantage of this rare opportunity to include this impressive-looking self-testimonial (above).

From every possible vantage point, whether on the ground, halfway up a building or even perched precariously on the rooftops, there was no holding back the enthusiastic crowds, who, along with the military contingents, patiently waited for the arrival of Lord Roberts.

The carriages containing all the invited guests continue to arrive at a designated area of Piccadilly where, having discharged their fares, are then turned around and despatched in the opposite direction.

With an escort of plumed horseback militiamen, Field Marshall Lord Roberts of Kandahar makes his jubilant appearance in Manchester's Piccadilly to a welcoming crowd of VIP's and dignitaries. Note the bunting and crowded balconies of the Albion Hotel and the tailoring establishment of Andrew Macbeth & Sons.

With this much clearer image of the Field Marshall, sitting upright in his carriage, what could be better than to allow one's thoughts to wander back in time, in order to bring back to life this wonderful Manchester pageantry.

To those who are familiar with Manchester's 'people of note', this photograph should prove invaluable. However, the emphasis of this picture lies in what must obviously be the last few remaining moments before the shrouded statue becomes exposed to the public.

Opposite above: Standing on a makeshift dais, Lord Roberts VC is captured on camera, moments after the unveiling ceremony.

Opposite below: No doubt at the request of the many photographers who would have been present, Lord Roberts VC poses with his fellow officials in front of Manchester's latest addition to its collection of monuments. The dignitaries included, from left to right: The Lord Mayor, the Lord Bishop, Onslow Ford, Lord Roberts and Sir F.F. Adams. Onslow Ford died just two months after this unveiling ceremony.

53

Reclining on her throne and with her back towards the hundreds of spectators on top of the Hospital Infirmary rooftop, Queen Victoria overlooks the proceedings as the day's ceremony draws near to conclusion.

Although Queen Victoria's statue was reportedly 'not the best sculptor that Onslow Ford had created', these two views contradict that opinion by the way it majestically stands out against the old and worn looking Infirmary. Looking from the Piccadilly esplanade towards the distant Albion Hotel, it is possible to see all the different kinds of horse carriages as they wait in line at Piccadilly's well-known taxi terminal.

On what was to be his last visit to Manchester, King Edward VII arrived in the city on 5 July 1909. Although staying as a guest of Lord Derby at Liverpool's Knowsley Hall, he was nevertheless in the Lancashire area in order to perform two important duties. One of those commitments included taking the royal salute at the Royal (Military) Tournament at Worsley, and, on the following day, 6 July, performing the grand Opening Ceremony of the new Manchester Infirmary on Oxford Road, Manchester. Previously, the King had visited Manchester in 1905, and again in 1887 when, as Prince Edward, he performed the opening of the Royal Jubilee Exhibition. While the weather appeared to have been favourable for the Royal Tournament on 5 July, the following day's visit to Manchester was much wetter.

In order of sequence, this photograph highlights the moment prior to the mounted troops taking the 'salute' on 5 July, with the King and his Queen looking down from the podium.

Inspired by his newly acquired fame, i.e., 'By Royal Command', Robert Banks went on to produce an album of the whole of the King's visit, which was later presented to the King.

This is one of the photographs taken by Robert Banks as the King's motor vehicle made its way along Oxford Road towards the new Manchester Infirmary. On this day, 6 July 1909, the Manchester weather had started out with overcast skies, as seen in this view of the cheering bystanders. However, by the time King Edward VII had arrived at the front gates of the Infirmary, the heavens opened, much to the dismay of the organisers, who, had worked for weeks in order to ensure the success of the grand opening of the Infirmary. From the time the building was declared 'open', Manchester Infirmary became officially known as the Manchester Royal Infirmary, or, more commonly, the 'Manchester Royal'.

7

MARCHES & RALLIES

During the year of 1869, Manchester, along with neighbouring Ashton-under-Lyne, formed a society which went by the name 'The Sons of Temperance Movement', with its main aim focussed on preventing men, women and children from drinking alcohol. Or, to put it another way, to promote and encourage abstinence from the evils of alcoholic potions.

The Temperance Movement, a national as well as international organisation, had been around for a number of years with powerful and influential support from other nations, and not least from the American continent. This fact is reflected in the wording of the Manchester and Ashton-under-Lyne marching banners, with one such banner proclaiming: 'Grand Division of the National Division of The Sons of Temperance'. Soon after the inauguration of this society came the women's contribution to the great cause, a title, which went by the name of: 'Manchester Grand Union of Daughters of Temperance'.

The following photographs illustrate the great depth of feeling by members of the alliance against alcohol when, during 1902, there was a parliamentary debate on the Licensing Bill. Taking full advantage of the publicity surrounding the proposed improvements to the licensing law, the Temperance Society paraded through the city streets at every opportunity. One of the amendments to the Bill was to penalise anyone found drunk while in charge of children.

Apart from the fact that this view shows a men-only parade marching in Albert Square, most temperance parades were led by women protestors, and for very good reason.

Stern-faced and determined-looking, these representatives from the Women's Temperance movement march through the city in 1902.

Mothers, daughters and sons seem to be the theme for this group of marchers near to the Manchester Town Hall. Judging by the appearance of the lady beneath the banner, a fainting session seems to be imminent. Wonder if a drop of brandy from a spectator would be allowed?!

To the accompaniment of male stewards and a brass band, this 1902 women's contingent marches proudly into Albert Square, where, later, a meeting of temperance workers will unite.

Someone somewhere will no doubt be able to add names to the people who were involved in this Suffragette march, which appears to have taken place on Princess Street. My own theory is that it was a WSPU March organised by Christabel Pankhurst in 1909, probably around the time when Emily Davidson, a convicted suffragette, was released from Strangeways Prison following her month-long ordeal.

In keeping with what appears to have been his lifetime philosophy of being in the right place at the right time, Robert Banks was on hand to photograph this Miners' Demonstration rally in 1901 at Southport.

8

A MISCELLANY OF PHOTOGRAPHS

On what appears to be a cold day, the bearded Manchester Lord Mayor John Royle wraps up warm alongside his travelling companion, Prime Minister Arthur J. Balfour. They are about to leave Albert Square en route to the new Manchester School of Technology on Sackville Street, where, on 15 October 1902, Prime Minister Balfour declared the building 'open'.

On 29 September 1900, the Right Honourable A.J. Balfour, Member of Parliament for Manchester East, paid a visit to the home of Manchester City Football Club. Together with his secretary, they watched the match between Manchester City and Stoke City Football Club. The final score was: Manchester City (2) Stoke City (0), with the goals coming from Meredith and Davies. Photographed by Robert Banks, this view shows the Rt Hon. A.J. Balfour in conversation with the Manchester City captain Billy Meredith before kick-off.

This view of the terraces at Manchester City football ground shows the dapper-looking A.J. Balfour with his secretary.

By the early 1900s, Manchester's Automobile Club began to gain momentum, albeit amongst the elitist minority who could afford such luxury. In the words of Robert Banks, relating to these two rare photographs, the first reads: 'The Manchester Automobile Club in the park (view taken from the terrace) of Willington Hall, Tarporley. Special invitation of Mr Tomlinson MP and Mrs Tomlinson.'

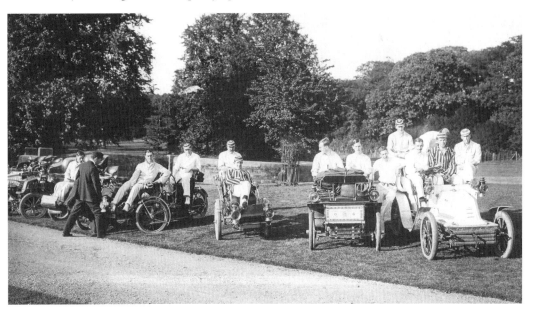

Again quoting Robert Banks, this second view reads: 'While the members of the Manchester Automobile Club were at tea with Mr and Mrs Tomlinson, of Willington Hall, their motors were invaded by a gentlemanly crowd of cricketers.'

When the great Barnum and Bailey's Circus visited Manchester in 1897, and, as a means of gaining as much publicity as possible for their Easter time performances, they organised grand parades along the main thoroughfares of the city. In this photograph, which was taken at Old Trafford, near to the canal swing bridge, a themed parade of what appears to be knights in armour pass along a crowded road.

This unusual photograph shows a line of forty horses, which are being driven by one man.

During the 1860s, not only was Manchester a garrison town but also the headquarters of what was then known as the Northern Garrison, an area stretching from Newcastle-on-Tyne in the north, to as far south as Birmingham and Weedon.

Manchester's two main troop barracks were situated close to the Deansgate area, where one was adjacent to the garrison Church of St George's in Hulme, whilst the other establishment was on the Regent Road area of Salford. At the Chester Road Barracks the resident military personnel included a volunteer regiment of infantrymen and a cavalry regiment.

How very proud the little boy must have felt in this photograph, standing in front of his father together with the other fourteen officers. The pose for this Robert Banks photograph was at the Chester Road building (main entrance) of the Twelfth Royal Lancers.

This 1890s photograph features a rank and file parade of Lancers on the parade ground of Hulme Barracks.

To the trained eye, there is something unusual about this article, published by the *Manchester Evening News* in 1884. On closer inspection the initial E, instead of R. Banks becomes apparent, as does the change of address. The reason behind both of these issues is a set of circumstances that befell Robert Banks, the first of which was a bankruptcy order, which forced Robert to trade under his wife's name and to move his business premises. During the same year, a second disaster struck when Emma, his beloved wife, died of Bright's disease. However, with the support of his three grown-up children, Robert managed to survive his ordeal and, as history has proved, he continued as Manchester's most prominent photographer.

This advert refers to the newly opened photographic business of Robert Banks and is believed to have come from a copy of the *Oldham Chronicle* dated 1870.

Opposite: The annual training camp of the West Yorkshire Rifle Volunteers (WYRV's) was held at a venue known as 'Pots and Pans', a hilly district above Greenfield. It was there, during 1874, that Robert Banks made a photographic record of the activities of the 'Volunteers' having received a commission to do so by their leader, Major Collins, who, having interrupted Robert Banks's imminent move to his new Manchester headquarters, requested a compilation of the twenty or so pictures in album form. From a historical point of view, Robert Banks's Upper mill premises continued trading for a few more years, and it was only when the remainder of his family moved to Manchester that he ceased his connections with the Saddleworth area.

Bearing a resemblance to a troop of soldiers in the American Civil War, the WYRV's pose outside their HQ tent while waiting for Robert Banks to complete his picture taking. Major Collins is seen sitting down in front of his men, while on the back row, fourth from the right, is Rifleman Buckley, who, this author believes, was related to Robert Banks's wife Emma, formerly Emma Buckley.

Behind this second view of the Rifle Volunteer troop lies a mystery that to date remains unsolved. Apart from the central figure of Major Collins and the paunchy Dr Lockwood with his funny-looking hat, there are two other gentlemen whose appearance in the picture comes as a great surprise. One, seated to the left of Major Collins, is the 5th Earl of Dartmouth, William Legge, while on the back row immediately behind the Major, is his son, the Hon. Charles Legge. At the time of this photograph, it is believed that Lord Dartmouth was an honorary Colonel of the South Staffordshire Volunteer Battalion, whereas his son, Henry Charles, was serving as an officer in the Coldstream Guards.

On 22 January 1901, General Sir Redvers Buller VC made an appearance in the city of Manchester in order to open a grand fête in aid of the Soldiers and Sailors Families Association. It was reported that an extra 500 policemen had been drafted into the city in order to control the masses that had turned out to lay eyes on the famous General.

General Buller VC had become an overnight hero on the South African battlefield on 28 March 1879, when he was thirty-nine years of age. It was recorded that while being pursued by Zulu warriors, Lt-Col Buller rescued the captain of a horse infantry by carrying him on his own horse to safety. Again on the same day and in similar circumstances, he carried another soldier whose horse had been killed in action. By the end of the day, and just yards away from an approaching army of Zulu warriors, he yet again rescued a trooper.

Sir Redvers Buller VC, having departed his carriage, pauses for the camera before making his way into the Manchester Town Hall. To the right are Father Bernard Vaughan of Liverpool, Miss Buller and the Manchester Lord Mayor.

Reunited with their carriage, following a luncheon with the Lord Mayor, the General and Mrs Buller begin their short ride to St James Hall on Oxford Street, where they opened a Victorian fête. Also included in the General's schedule was a meeting with Manchester veterans of the Crimea. Having successfully accomplished his itinerary, Sir Redvers Buller VC then left Manchester to travel to Garswood Hall in Cheshire, as guests of Lord and Lady Gerard.

On 27 April 1901, a crowd of 30,000 spectators watched the football match replay between Tottenham Hotspur and Sheffield United at Burnden Park. In an earlier meeting at Crystal Palace, and in front of a crowd of 110,000 people, the match ended in a hotly disputed 2-2 draw. The reason for the small attendance at Bolton was the Railway Company's refusal to issue cheap tickets. It was recorded that the receipts from the 19,000 spectators who paid admission at the gates amounted to £1,197 6s 9d.

The Tottenham Hotspur goalkeeper is seen here retrieving the ball in front of the goalmouth. With their win over Sheffield United, Tottenham became the first non-league football team to win the coveted FA Cup.

Along with Robert Banks, three other photographers are positioned ready to capture the start of this 1901 bicycle race at the Fallowfield Manchester Athletics Ground. The stadium was best known for its association with the Manchester Wheelers Club and Reg Harris, after whom the stadium was named. Of note is the fact that Robert Banks was also responsible for taking the photographs of both the 1893 and 1899 FA Cup matches at the same location.

This garden party was held at Craven Terrace, Sale, near Manchester, in 1909. Sadly nothing else is known about the event.

This is one of Robert Banks's mystery photographs. It has no date or description and therefore one can only speculate as to its identity. The photography however, bears all the usual hallmarks of a Robert Banks production.

The new and exciting era of electric tramcars in Manchester began on Thursday, 6 June 1901 in front of the Town Hall. For this special occasion, and as if to present a new aspect of modern-day transport for the city, no horse-drawn vehicles were aloud in, or anywhere near, Albert Square. The line-up of electric vehicles were decorated from head to toe in garlands of flowers as they awaited their moment in time, a pause, as it were, before the looming twentieth century brought them, and the associated noise and chaos, a step closer.

On the stroke of 11.30 a.m., the loud ringing of the tram bells heralded the first city tram service to Cheetham Hill, a journey costing tuppence for a one-way service. The first tramcar, transporting the Lord Mayor of Salford and the Lord Mayor of Manchester, made its first stop at the new tram sheds at Queen's Road. There, with a gold key, the Manchester Lord Mayor declared the building open. Following the completion of the return journey, the 180 guests were invited to a Town Hall banquet.

This view of the electric tramcar line-up in Albert Square shows tram 118 awaiting the signal for the epic journey to begin.

On 25 July 1900, and on what was one of the hottest days of the year, a famous and wealthy duchess arrived in Manchester with the aim of 'officially' opening an extension wing to the Charter Street Ragged School. This lady of note was the Duchess of Sutherland, whose family home was at Dunrobin Castle, Sutherland. Her other family estates included Trentham, Lilleshall and the Lancaster House in London. Following a train journey to Manchester from Stoke-on-Trent, the Duchess, together with her private secretary Miss Lucy James, continued the remainder of the journey to Angel Meadow by horse and carriage. In visiting the Charter Street Ragged School, the Staffordshire 'Potteries' Duchess had now joined the ranks of a long line of illustrious celebrities who had previously visited the Angel Meadow School. They included the Earl of Shaftesbury, General Booth, General Gordon, Dr Barnardo, Winston Churchill, Mr A.J. Balfour and the American Evangelists Moody and Sankey.

In order to capture the moment of the Duchess's arrival in Angel Meadow, Robert Banks positioned his camera at the north end of Ashley Lane, thus giving him a view of the ragged school to the right and St Michael's Flags to the left. For whatever reason, Robert decided to turn his camera on the local residents. In monetary terms, Robert must have realised that there was no value in the picture, as no one in the photograph would have been able to pay for a printed copy.

Opposite: At a time when Britain was the world's richest nation, this photograph reveals just how severe the degree of poverty was in the country's major cities at the time. Here, with their bare feet and ill-fitting rags, stand a group of Manchester residents who know no other life than wondering where the next meal will come from. Most certainly, Robert Banks deserves the credit for producing this iconic image, a photograph which sums up the daily struggle for many families in Victorian Britain.

Cascaded with bunting and with every available space in and out of the buildings full to capacity, Angel Meadow lays on its welcome for the Duchess of Sutherland. In this view, the Duchess acknowledges the spectators before stepping out of the carriage.

Opposite above: It would appear that this photograph of the (old) Manchester Infirmary in Piccadilly was taken from Mosley Street, owing to the absence of the usual perimeter seat benches and the familiar line up of horse-drawn taxis. Manchester Infirmary and Lunatic Asylum had proudly stood on this (Daub-Hole) Piccadilly site for 150 years or so, prior to removing to Oxford Road in 1909, when in that same year it was renamed the Manchester Royal Infirmary.

The now empty shell of the city's landmark Infirmary is seen standing in isolation prior to its demolition in 1910, although one of its most famous features, the 'cupola' clock, minus its hands, still gazes down from its tower. The advertising signs on the building read: 'Bricks, Slates, Stones and All Materials On Sale – Samuel Whittall' and 'Contractor – George H Jones – Apply On The Job.'

Opposite below: Pictured in this early 1900s photograph are a group of women inmates on the morning of their release from Manchester's Strangeways Prison. The Southall Street prison entrance has, as is noticeable, been taken over by several well-dressed evangelists from the 'City Mission', who are not only on hand to give good advice to the wrongdoers, but are also there to invite them to a coffee tavern, where they will encourage the women to sign the pledge. The Manchester City Mission, which was formed in 1837, and whose roots go back to the 'Glasgow' Mission, inspired by David Nasmith, was one of Manchester and Salford's leading charities. The 'City Mission' has survived to this day, and is involved in such benevolences as 'drop-in' centres and night shelters, along with various other projects.

During the year 1897, a merger took place between two of the country's leading armament manufacturers; Sir W.G. Armstrong of Newcastle-upon-Tyne and Sir Joseph Whitworth of Openshaw, Manchester. The names of these two precision engineering craftsmen, i.e. Armstrong Whitworth & Co, became recognised throughout the world, not only as arms manufacturers, but also as shipbuilders. In the early 1900s the company was involved in the building of countless numbers of warships', amongst which were vessels for the Imperial Russian Navy and the Imperial Japanese Navy. In later years the company involved itself in steam train manufacture, aeroplanes, and motor car manufacturing, notably the Armstrong Siddeley automobile. Sir Joseph Whitworth, a Stockport-born man, who died while convalescing at Monte Carlo in 1887, aged eighty-three, left a fortune of legacies to the city of Manchester, amongst which was the Whitworth Art Gallery and Museum.

Just imagine if you can, the skill, precision and manoeuvrability that was required in transporting this giant 29-ton gun barrel from the Openshaw Works, to the docks at Trafford Wharf. It was reported at that time that fourteen horses were required to pull the contraption along the cobbled thoroughfares of the city. As the gun arrives at the dockside in 1901, it proudly displays its 'Manchester' logo, whereas above it, along the barrel, is another marking with the engraving: 'Sir W.G. Armstrong Whitworth & Co. 9-2 B.L. Wire Gun.'

Overseen by the bowler-hatted foremen, the precious cargo is slowly lowered onto the waiting vessel, at which point the gun's destination becomes apparent. Printed on the mounting that is awaiting the all-important gun is the inscription: 'H.M.S. London.' - 35 – AFT.' There is another inscription detailing the weight capacity, which reads: '43Tons, 19Cwts, 3Qtrs, and 0Lbs'. This gun was one of four that were made for the newly-built

battleship HMS London which, having been launched at Portsmouth in 1899, was completed in 1902. The task of transporting the gun down the Manchester Ship Canal to Woolwich Arsenal was awarded to Messrs Fletcher Woodhill.

When looking at this Robert Banks photograph, which was taken close to the junctions of Church Road, Ford Lane and Royle Green Road, one immediately becomes aware of the slow pace of life that was so often portrayed by our great-grandparents.

This photograph was taken on the banks of the Manchester Ship Canal. The author's guess would be Eastham.

In what was seen as a very unusual visit, an assembly of Colonial Premiers visited the city of Manchester on the 3rd and 4th of May 1907. Among the many VIP's were Sir Robert Bond of Newfoundland, Sir Joseph Ward of New Zealand, Mr Robert Moor of Natal, General Louis Botha of the Transvaal, and the UK representatives of the Colonial Office, Winston Churchill and Captain Guest. Whilst advertising the 'visit' as a great success, another local newspaper gave a very different point of view: 'A dull and apathetic visit' was their summing-up, 'with very few crowds and very little bunting, apart from the Imperial Hotel, headquarters of the Manchester United Football Club, where, written on a huge banner hanging from the first-floor window, were the words: "Why Can't We Always Be United".'

While in the process of starting-out for their day's itinerary, Robert Banks managed to capture the majority of the Premiers in this group photograph outside the Midland Hotel in Manchester. What is so interesting about this picture are the unusual circumstances surrounding Winston Churchill and General Louis Botha of South Africa. As a war correspondent travelling with British soldiers in the Transvaal in 1899, an enemy Boer soldier captured Winston Churchill. Some years later, whilst visiting London, General Botha came face-to-face with Winston Churchill and, as a result of talking about their experiences, General Botha revealed himself as being the very soldier who had taken him prisoner.

At some point later in the day, the Colonial Premiers paid a visit to the Downing Street premises of the Manchester and Salford Equitable Co-operative Society where, following an address, they then made their way to the Manchester Town Hall to attend a banquet that was being held in their honour.

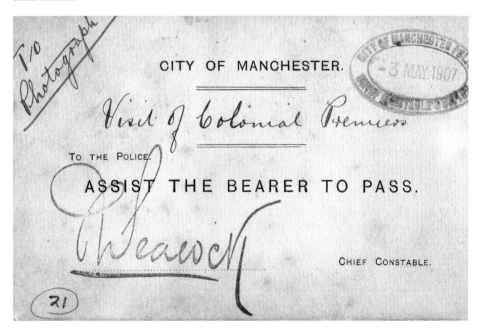

Yet another delightful item of memorabilia is this official 'pass' issued to Robert Banks, which, together with its date and details, becomes self-explanatory. On the reverse of this 'pass' is one of Robert Banks's wax seals, advertising his Fountain Street business premises. However, what is more eye-catching is his wording, which refers to him as supplying photographs 'By Command' to His Majesty the King.

The idea of creating a training ship was down to Liverpool ship owner John Clint, who, having felt the need to create an opportunity to train local destitute and orphaned boys to become merchant seamen, pleaded with the Admiralty for their help and involvement. With a sum of money from James Bibby's shipping line, together with a loaned frigate-ship from Her Majesty's Navy, the training ship *Indefatigable* came into existence in 1864.

Most probably at the request of the Manchester and Salford 'Boys and Girls Refuges', Robert Banks travelled to Liverpool and the Wirral in 1898 in order to photograph the training ship *Indefatigable*, moored in a stretch of water off Rock Ferry, known locally as 'The Sloyne'. Once in the hands of the Refuges trustees, this photograph would have served as a proud reminder of Manchester's contribution to the cause of ridding the streets of its destitute children in favour of providing alternatives, such as training to become merchant sailors. Whilst photographing the Mersey-based *Indefatigable*, Robert Banks took this opportunity to capture the profiles of the other three 'wooden-wall' training ships, *Akbar*, *Clarence* and HMS *Conway*. Little did he realise that within twelve months of photographing the *Clarence*, it would end up at the bottom of the River Mersey.

9

MANCHESTER VIEWS

Manchester University in the early 1900s.

According to Robert Banks, 'Bogart Hole Clough' became the latest of Manchester's acquisitions. It was a park, standing in 170 acres and had a statue commemorating the Lancashire poet Ben Brierley.

When Smithfield Market moved to the Openshaw district of Manchester at the turn of the century, it took with it an unimaginable wealth of memories, both from its traders, the general public, and the former Swan Street headquarters.

This rather unusual photograph was one of two Robert Banks views of Spring Gardens post office in central Manchester. There appears to be a total of twenty-two telephonists, each sat on their high chairs, while in the middle of the sparse-looking room sit two stern-faced overseers who are sat in such a position that they are able to keep an eye on either side of the exchange.

Taken approximately 110 years ago, these two views represent what would have been an everyday scenario along the industrialized sidings of the Trafford Wharf section of the Manchester Ship Canal. Of note is the convenient appearance of the SS *Manchester City* merchant ship, which is shown here discharging its cargo of grain.

One of Robert Banks's famous and well-publicised photographs is this view of the 1893 FA Cup Final between Wolverhampton Wanderers and Everton. It was played at the Fallowfield Athletics Stadium in Manchester, where the final score was 1-0 in Wolves's favour. On that day, 25 March, it was reported that the stadium, normally of 15,000 capacity, became swelled by an estimated crowd of 60,000. Little wonder that almost two thirds of the onlookers hardly saw anything.

The next big football occasion at Fallowfield occurred in March 1899, when Sheffield United played Liverpool in an FA Cup semi-final. As a result of a pitch invasion from the terraces, the match had to be abandoned, and, when the two clubs met at Burnden Park for the second time, it ended in a 4-4 draw. The final decider, which was played at the Baseball Ground, ended in a victory for Sheffield United.

It would appear that Robert Banks had positioned his tripod on the actual racecourse in order to photograph what was one of the first meetings being held at the new Manchester Racecourse at Castle Irwell in 1902. Strangely enough, this wasn't the first time that horse racing had been held at Castle Irwell. Records show that this same course had been operating for a period of twenty years between 1847 and 1867 before being relocated to Weaste, another Salford suburb. Not until 1902 did the 'Races' return to Castle Irwell and there they stayed until their demise in 1963, after which the 'course' and land became part of Salford University.

No book on old Manchester would be complete, without mention of one of the city's oldest establishments, Chethams School. Commonly known as 'Chet's', it was founded in 1653 by Humphrey Chetham as a 'charity' hospital-school for the poor, whereas today it continues to receive worldwide acclaim for its Library and School of Music.

During the excavation and construction of the Manchester Ship Canal, the entrepreneurial Robert Banks made many visits to the site in order to capture on camera the important beginnings of this immense undertaking. In particular, he took many photographs in the Barton area of Eccles, where the Barton Aqueduct was being built. No doubt Robert Banks timed the taking of this view of the completed Barton Aqueduct in order to capture the horse-drawn coal barge.

Suspended in mid-air, this coal wagon appears to be in the process of being loaded aboard a waiting ship at Manchester Docks. As with the previous picture, this photograph was taken prior to 1900.

When it comes to Manchester views, there is one venue that stands out more than any other, and that is Belle Vue. It meant many things to many different people, whether it was animals, entertainment, band concerts, circuses or speedway. However, so far as banqueting events were concerned, and, owing to the size of its great hall, Belle Vue was seen as the place in which to hold business dinners, social dinners, wedding parties and other celebrations. This Robert Banks photograph is confirmation of the popularity of the renowned Belle Vue banqueting, although, regrettably, this particular event is unknown.

This Robert Banks picture of the All Saints' Church, which used to stand on the corner of Oxford Road and Cavendish Street, brings to mind the famous painting by Pierre Valette, who used this same view of the horse cabs as his main theme. Now a park, this area of the city will always be associated with L.S. Lowry and P.A. Valette, the former having been an art student in Valette's art class at the building on Cavendish Street.

The Withy Grove area of Manchester, a site that had been associated with street trading since the nineteenth century, including its famous 'Hen Market', came to a sad ending in the early 1970s when construction began on the Manchester Arndale Centre. Seen in this photograph is the reputed site of the old Rovers Return public house, while opposite would have stood Manchester's acclaimed oldest pub, The Seven Stars.

When it came to choosing a subject for the expanding market of postcard manufacturing, the late nineteenth-century Manchester photographers, including Robert Banks, would have invariably given consideration to this historic-looking building on Long Millgate, close to Chetham's School. This peculiar-shaped building known as Poets Corner, a construction dating back 300 years, owed its fame to a Lancashire poet by the name of Critchley Prince. Since then, the building was used for a variety of businesses, including a pub by the name of Sun Inn, a sweet shop, a bakers shop, a book shop and an antiques and curiosity shop.

In terms of perfection, Robert Banks would probably have been well satisfied with the result of this Manchester Cathedral view.

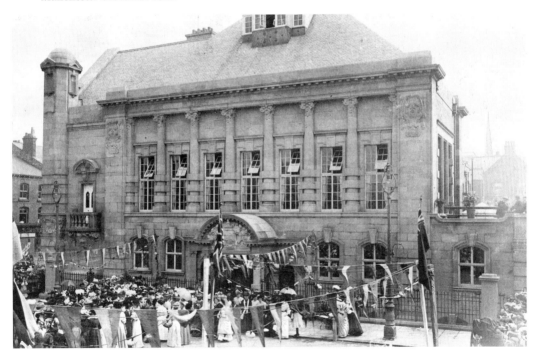

With no sign of any males, apart from the rooftop onlookers, this scene in front of the newly opened Leigh Town Hall is reminiscent of a Suffragette meeting. It is worth noting that when taking this photograph, Robert Banks had returned to the very district in which he had been born.

10

ROBERT BANKS

Frenches, Greenfield.

The beginnings of Robert Banks's career as a photographer began in a small hamlet of Greenfield, known locally as 'Frenches', and it was there in a small studio that he set himself up as a photographer-come-picture-frame maker. This pre-First World War photograph was taken on Chew Valley Road, a thoroughfare that Robert Banks would have been very familiar with. Unlike the old days when the district came under the jurisdiction of the Yorkshire West Riding, Greenfield, a part of the Saddleworth parish of Oldham, is now included as a part of Greater Manchester.

'Carte de Visite's', or Visiting Cards, which originated in France, became extremely popular with the Victorian photographers of this country, especially from the 1880s onwards, when, in the new era of seaside holidaying, there were fortunes waiting to be made. Right from the start of his business empire, Robert Banks had concentrated his efforts on the bread and butter income that came from his 'Carte de Visite' trade. These two featured samples, also known as 'cabinet cards', were a typical example of Robert Banks's achievements.

Pictured here are just four examples of the kind of information and artistry that appeared on the reverse side of the thousands of Robert Banks's 'Carte de Visite's'. In this modern-day era of family researching, plus internet technology, it would be quite feasible for a family to stumble across distant relatives who had been photographed by Robert Banks, especially if they'd had connections with Blackpool, Manchester or Saddleworth. Of special note are the various business addresses used by Robert Banks.

Having lived and worked in Greenfield at a young age, Robert Banks became accustomed to observing the many thousands of visitors from all over the country who made an annual pilgrimage to the town he lived in. They, the inquisitive and the morbid, were there to visit the two places that had now become shrines. The story behind this seemingly annual mass-migration goes as far back as 1832, when an innkeeper and his son, William and Thomas Bradbury, were brutally and savagely murdered inside their public house, the Moorcock Inn. Such was the barbaric nature of the crime that one of the corpses was unrecognisable. Two suspects were later apprehended but, due to lack of evidence, were released. To date, the crime remains unsolved.

Having digested his knowledge of the event and taken note of how the sightseers used to flock to the Greenfield churchyard and Moorcock Inn, the entrepreneurial Robert Banks, in 1882, decided to use the fiftieth anniversary (jubilee) as a way of feeding the curiosity of the thousands of visitors who still journeyed to Greenfield.

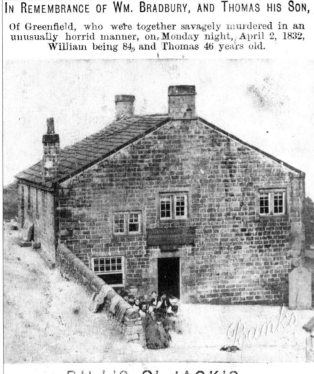

IN REMEMBRANCE OF WM. BRADBURY, AND THOMAS HIS SON,

Of Greenfield, who were together savagely murdered in an unusually horrid manner, on Monday night, April 2, 1832, William being 84, and Thomas 46 years old.

BILL'S O' JACK'S.

Throughout the land, wherever news is read,
Intelligence of their sad death has spread ;
Those who now talk of far-famed Greenfield hills,
Will think of Bill o' Jack's and Tom o' Bill's.

Such interest did their tragic end excite,
That, ere they were removed from human sight,
Thousands on thousands came to see
The bloody scene of the catastrophe.

One house, one business, and one bed,
And one most shocking death they had ;
One funeral came, one inquest passed,
And now one grave they have at last.

R. BANKS
ARTIST

75ª MARKET ST
MANCHESTER

Probably one of his best 'Carte de Visite's' and one that must have been profitable was Robert Banks's creation of this Bill's o'Jack's commemorative card. The Moorcock Inn, which he photographed for this occasion, and which was still attracting visitors 100 years later, was demolished in 1937. A local schoolteacher was believed to have been the author of the poem at the time of the murders.

NOTICE EXTENDED,

From January 22nd to February 17th, 1880.

The following advertisement was formerly for 21 days, but in consequence of so many HUNDREDS of inquiries made to R. BANKS by letter, post card, messenger, &c., asking him if he would favour them with a sitting for their Photographs at one-half the usual price, providing they send in their names during the advertisement of half-price, and PAY WHEN THEY COME to have their Photograph taken. The following is a copy of

THE REPLY— "If not convenient for you to sit during the short time of this advertisement, you can send to me, by post or otherwise, 2/6, 3/9, or 5/3 according to the kind you require, and I will give you a receipt for it, and enter it in the books so that you can have a sitting for your Photographs at any time during the summer months of 1880."

All Orders per post must be accompanied with cash and stamped envelope for reply.

Carte-de-Visite and Cabinet Photographs by R. BANKS will be charged only ONE-HALF THE USUAL PRICE.

For example, those formerly charged 5/- per dozen will be 2/6, those charged 7/6 will be 3/9, and those charged 10/6 will be 5/3. Other prices charged at the same rate, that is to say, one-half the usual price.

Should any person be desirous of having another dozen from any of the Negatives previously taken at any of his Studies, they can be supplied at one-half the usual price during the term of this notice.

JUVENILES.—Where only a small amount of pocket money is allowed to meet these young people's wants, 500 dozen will be issued to boys and girls over seven and under twelve years of age at 2/- per dozen.

Should any Lady or Gentlemen have a Carte-de-Visite of themselves or any relative or friend, they can have it copied and One Dozen Cartes printed from it for 3/9.

R. BANKS wishes it to be clearly understood that all work done during this notice will be equally as well finished as that at the usual price.

R. BANKS, PHOTOGRAPHER,
73A, MARKET STREET,
CORNER OF NEW BROWN STREET;
1, NEW CROSS;
AND AT HIS RESIDENCE—
REMBRANDT HOUSE, ALEXANDRA PARK, MANCHESTER.

The above Prices quoted are meant as an advertising medium for 1880. See "Evening Mail" and "Evening News" every day.

Left: In this very extensive advertisement in the 'City Jackdaw' publication, Robert Banks appears to have left no stone unturned in his endeavours to encourage its readers to part with their money. His tactics seem to suggest that his photographic studios haven't lived up to expectations, hence this seemingly last-ditch effort to reverse the company's fortunes.

Below: This rare and unusual postcard, which bears a hand-written message from Robert Banks to his picture-frame maker, gives an insight into some of his business dealings. It is also a significant piece of Manchester's history, especially in connection with King Edward's visit to the city in 1906. Also of note is Robert Banks new address at Fountain Street, having moved from his long-term premises that were situated in the Royal Hotel building on Market Street.

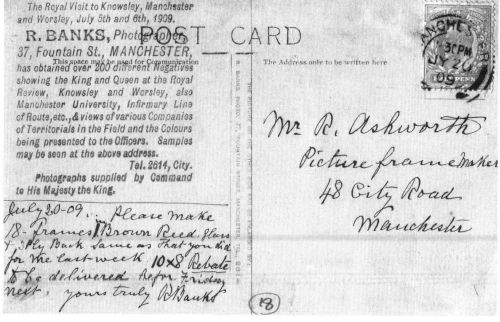

AFTERWORD

If your appetite has been wetted by these Robert Banks images, then the good news is that there are many more of his photographs still waiting to be discovered. For instance, Robert Banks produced an album of the 1902 Preston Guild. He also travelled to London, where he compiled a set of photographs recording the official reception given to Captain Lambert and his crewmembers, of 'Ladysmith' fame. Another collection he produced was in connection with Buffalo Bill's 'Sioux Indian' visit to Manchester and Salford in 1887 and 1903.

Since I am considering donating my Robert Banks collection to a worthwhile trust, I would like to appeal to those members of the public who would be interested in either donating or selling their Robert Banks memorabilia.

Finally, I would like to thank the *Manchester Evening News* for their kind support in appealing for information. Without their co-operation this book would not have been possible.

Sincerely,
James Stanhope-Brown

Other titles published by The History Press

The Golden Years of Manchester Picture Houses
Memories of the Silver Screen 1900–1970
DEREK J. SOUTHALL

This delightful collection of memories from the golden age of cinema in Manchester features archive images recalling courting days and war-time air raids, the stars, the staff and all the magic of the silver screen. 'When my husband and I were courting, we used to go to the Rivoli cinema in Gorton. It was a very big old cinema, and we soon learned that it was advisable to keep your feet up on the seat in front. It was not unusual, if you kept your feet on the floor, for "things" to run over your feet.'

978 0 7524 4981 4

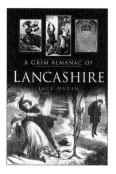

A Grim Almanac of Lancashire
JACK NADIN

A Grim Almanac of Lancashire is a day-by-day catalogue of 365 ghastly tales from around the county dating from the twelfth to the twentieth centuries. Full of dreadful deeds, macabre deaths, strange occurrences and heinous homicides, this almanac explores the darker side of the county's past. This compilation contains diverse tales of highwaymen, murderers, bodysnatchers, poachers, witches, rioters and rebels, as well as accounts of old lock-ups, prisons, bridewells and punishments.

978 0 7524 5684 3

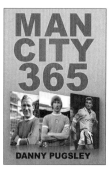

Man City 365
DANNY PUGSLEY

The phrase 'typical city' is synonymous with the life and times of Manchester City Football Club. The history of the club has veered between triumph and tragedy, providing joy and tears in equal measure. *Man City 365* chronicles, in a day by day account, the most significant events and landmarks from every day of the year. Charting classic matches, records, signings and the most beloved players to the downright bizarre, the book provides a fascinating and humorous insight and testament into the club's place in the footballing world.

978 0 7524 5782 6

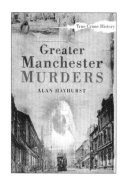

Greater Manchester Murders
ALAN HAYHURST

Contained within the pages of this book are the stories behind some of the most notorious murders in the history of Greater Manchester. They include the case of cat burglar Charlie Peace, who killed twenty-year-old PC Nicolas Cock in Seymour Grove, and only confessed after he had been sentenced to death and the death of Police Sergeant Charles Brett, who stuck bravely to his post despite an armed attack on his prison van by the 'Manchester Martyrs'.

978 0 7509 5091 6

Visit our website and discover thousands of other History Press books.

www.thehistorypress.co.uk